THE REAL REASON WHY YOU STUCK WHERE YOU ARE

DEDICATION

This book is dedicated with love and respect to the three most important people in my life:

Zanele Dlamini:

You have been nothing but a supermom to me, loving me and supporting me even when I did things that didn't make sense and didn't agree with me. All you ever did was give me unconditional love which has made me want to make you proud of me.

Nkosinathi Dlamini:

The toughest man I know, the man who did anything and everything for his family. I have never heard you complain. You are the just the pillar of our family and I'm blessed to have you as my father. Instead of preaching to me, you have clearly showed me with action on how to take care of your family and protect them.

Ayanda Dlamini

The younger who always thinks of himself as being older than me, the early physical fights which ALWAYS resulted in you crying and mom shouting at me. Now you have become my closest friend that I look up to because you inspire me to be a better person.

TABLE OF CONTENTS

INTRODUCTION 1

OPPORTUNITY VS SUCCESS 8

LOST OPPORTUNITIES 13

VEHICLES OF OPPORTUNITY 19

JOB 20

SELF EMPLOYMENT OR JOB WITH SIDE HUSTLE 22

DUPLICATABLE BUSINESS 24

INCOME PRODUCING ASSETS 29

WHAT IT TAKES! 31

#1 SKILL 34

CONCLUSION 39

MY JOURNEY 40

APPRECIATION 43

THANK YOU AND APPRECIATION LIST 44

FIND ME 46

INTRODUCTION

"How did I get myself in this mess, situation and challenge?"

OPPORTUNITY!

That's one of the most valuable words in the English language. In this day and age that word has lost it's value mainly because we don't seem to understand it's true nature. Now why I say that?

Simply because we live average lives and are unhappy with our current economic affairs, how often does it happen that the money runs out before your next pay day?. I can guarantee you that it happens more often than not. If you fall in this category then I'm going to give you something called a "CONSCIOUS INTERUPT".

There is a category called "Middle Class" and particularly with the individuals in this category, everything looks rosy financially from a distance, but when you take a closer look at what's going on inside, the walls are closing in BIG TIME. Oprah interviewed

Robert Kyosaki and Robert called this category, "Looking good but going nowhere".

The fact is that the rich are still getting richer and the poor are getting even poorer, this statement has held true from the beginning of time and still holds true today.

WHY THOUGH?

Simple answer lies in this concept called Opportunity. The poor don't understand it, it's blind to them. The middle class seems to understand half of it but not the full picture because they settle with what they have and are never able to take full advantage of Opportunity. The rich and wealthy thrive on it, I mean why else would the gap keep growing? The rich and wealthy category know very well that you can't celebrate on yesterdays success and so they are always in constant search of new Opportunities out there and when they find them, they are able to take full advantage of them.

It's becomes a snowball effect over time because that's the Law of Momentum. Those in motion will carry on moving faster and faster and for those at a standstill will struggle to even get going. Those who currently don't have any Opportunities will struggle to even find one and if they do, it will be hard to execute yet those who are currently executing multiple Opportunities keep finding more and more and so on.

There is some great news though, once you find and execute an opportunity, the second one will be easier to find and execute. If you disciplined enough to stick to what works and not get bored along the way and you just repeat the process, then you will find yourself in momentum. This story reminds me of how the DC Superhero called "The Flash" used his speed to become a hero. He was terrified to save lives in the face of danger, then one day his comrade Superman told him to just save one life, of which The Flash did. He was surprised at how easy it was to save just one person, and he only focused on one person, then the next and the next. After an hour The Flash had saved over 100 lives because with each person saved, he gained confidence and got better at it. He didn't try fancy things, and kept it simple and repeated the process.

It's also the same with opportunity, start with one and FOCUS (Follow One Course Until Success) on it will you execute it and you carrying like that consistently over years, where you find yourself may be a pleasant place indeed financially because that's what this book is about. Figuring out what opportunities out there which can us out of where we are.

To tell you the truth, you actually took the concept I stated above and let the law of momentum work for you, then you don't need to read the rest of the book because it's that simple, not easy but simple. Heres the roadmap, "Look for Opportunity, when you find it, take action steps to get it then you execute it. Repeat the process over and over, you never stop" The only thing that will be different with each situation is the size of the Opportunity being executed.

We live in an economic planet, so money is not kinder important, it's actually EXTREMELY important. The demand for money now is greater now than our parents and grandparents era. Life now is totally different, more competitive marketplace, technological advancements which require an ever growing list of skill sets etc. Due to such growth, our upbringings never got us fully prepared for the real world we live in now, even the school system is great but we aren't taught how to practically apply our knowledge so compete in the real world. So our upbringings put us in a heavy disadvantage to compete. We have amazing curriculums such Business Studies, English, History, Accounting, Science, Biology etc and if in High School we are given practical ways to apply our knowledge then the school system would serve us better and equip us for the real world.

The real world is a different ball game to school and tertiary. It's tougher, more competitive, cruel, unfair, rewarding provided you have the right combination of IQ and EQ skills and taking massive amounts of action. Society encourages us to go to school to get good grades, so that we become great employees who are great but society doesn't support the flip side which is entrepreneurship which creates those jobs. We all head out to look for jobs which are a type of Opportunity.

In this book we will keep concepts and example very simple and easy to understand. What is covered is here is not new information, it's thing you already know but presented in a different which practical and doable provided you keep it simple. We tend to over overcomplicate simple things and that why we never execute. "Complexity is the enemy of execution and execution is everything"

There are 4 vehicles of opportunity available out there. Think of as vehicle that can take you from point A to point B. Point A being your current financial status and Point B being Financial Freedom which is R50 million rand in assets which pay you passive income of 10% every month. That's an IDEAL SITUATION. Now where these vehicles differ is the time it takes to get your destination. So here are the 4 vehicles of opportunity:

1. JOB
2. SELF EMPLOYMENT OR JOB WITH A SIDE HUSTLE
3. DUPLICATABLE BUSINESS
4. INVESTMENTS

Let's further add to this example where Point A is Durban (DBN) and Point B is Johannesburg (JHB). If we have a journey from DBN to JHB, decisions have to be made as to which vehicle is most suited for the journey.

OPPORTUNITY VS SUCCESS

Everyone wants success, including myself but I personally haven't reached the financial success that I want so unfortunately I can't talk about something that I haven't achieved yet. Opportunity on the other hand is something I'm super familiar with. I had a problem of being stuck somewhere financially and I have been trying to figure out as to how to get the next level by identifying bigger opportunities. So this was a process I used to find out where I got lost on the roadmap to financial freedom and so I hope you able to benefit out of this process, you will be able to figure out yourself where you are on the roadmap and start charting your course towards financial freedom. There is always room for improvement so study deeply what I talk about here.

Since I had all this knowledge and experience, I had to create space for new information and skills. My glass was full of water which wasn't serving me anymore, so the first thing was to pour out that water and that's how space is created for new water or you could get a bigger glass which is to increase your capacity to take in more information and process it. Either or is perfect because you have to be open to absorb that fresh new knowledge and be willing to let go of the old ideas and beliefs which may have been the reason why you were stuck were you were. I know that was very true for me.

What I discovered long time ago is that life is not fair, actually I don't remember a time in history where it was fair. We know stories of people who had more advantages than the rest, some who have disadvantages worse than everyone else, and our current situation which probably we blame someone for. Best to stop pointing fingers and complaining, start taking 100% responsibility for your life, you would be amazed at how much control you get over your life when you adopt that mentality because it gears you up to take advantage of Opportunity.

Money makes the world go around and this books talks about the M word that people are so shy to admit. I want to make bunches of money and I'm often criticized for it because that person labeling me says I'm "Materialistic". How many people love money? If your answer is yes than this book is for you. When you get your money right, life gets easier, you better able to deal with sudden emergencies which weren't planned for, you better able to take care of your family, you can donate on a bigger scale, you live your dream house and dream car, explore the world and create a financial wall for your family and generations to come that's indestructible. Heck if those are your reason for wanting money, then I don't see how you are being materialistic.

There are those who are shy to admit that they want money and say "I just want to be comfortable with my nice house and two cars and family". There is definitely nothing wrong with that, but I do encourage you to do more than just comfortable because that means you thinking about the here and now moment. You are not thinking of securing the future for the generations to come. If you have the potential of making money than you need in this lifetime, then you have an obligation to make that amount. Take what you need for your comfy lifestyle and give the rest away to charity or investments which secure generational wealth.

This next exercise is painful. Take a moment to think of the Opportunities in the past which that you wish you took advantage but couldn't see at the that time it presented itself to you that by the time you realized it, the door was closed. Write that down. Now think, why that happened as to what was missing that caused you not to see it and also write that down. These are the opportunities that you know very well if you had spotted and took advantage off, your bank balance would have more zeros. Empty mind on paper so that you are aware of those reasons so you it doesn't repeat itself going forward into the future. Same goes with the opportunities that you took advantage off but didn't work out, write down those reason and also with the ones that worked because note down. You will notice a pattern of what works and what doesn't.

Stick to what works

LOST OPPORTUNITES

The best stories are your own because you understand them best and are able articulate to yourself on how to get better. I used to have something I would call "Avoidance behavior" where I would procrastinate on an important task to take advantage of opportunity, so much so that the door would eventually close. Guess what would follow, convincing myself that it wasn't important, wasn't for me, it wasn't meant to be, not my time yet, giving others a chance, I have a lot on my plate already, I don't have the time, I don't have the money. Sound familiar because this list is endless. Now I'm to catch myself when I fall into procrastination mode, but here's a story to show how my procrastination messed up great opportunity for me.

I was doing my 1st year at university. I had applied for the Allan Gray Orbis Foundation Scholarship, I was so motivated in the application process and interview process that I made it to the final round where we would compete against other finalists from other Universities. This was the ultimate scholarship because everyone wants to get into Allan Gray.

Little did I know that my two close friends also made it as finalists, Eish and when we are together, we can't take anything serious because as a unit we take everything as a joke. So things just went downhill from there because I allowed myself to get distracted and not take things serious, actually as a joke *(side note, my mom and dad will kill me when they see this part)*. This wasn't any ordinary camp, it was tough, intense and competitive which required a person to be fully engaged to each and every activity. The more we progressed with the activities the less I took part because I was to disengaged after the first 2 hours and that lasted for the next two days. By the time we were done I had rationalized to myself that this wasn't for me and as a resulted I didn't make it into ALLAN GRAY.

This is what happened, When a difficult task was presented to us, I simply had avoidance behavior by procrastinating through jokes as opposed to taking the tasks seriously and figuring out what needed to happen and taking an active participating role of which I talked myself out of it.

Here's the kicker, I was really disappointed that I didn't make it, I actually felt that they made a mistake that I didn't make it, maybe an admin error. I still think about it till this day.

What I should have done was declare to myself and prove it by tackling all the activities with my best effort and challenge myself because I do believe I would have made it had I done that, but that's a lost opportunity for me which I forever regret.

There is another pitfall that I would always prey to which is to RELAX when thing are going smooth. What this does is cut your momentum run to stand still.

I used to work for a Transport company where I was operations manager for. I moved operations to the Richards Bay where company had very minimal business there. When I got there, I saw all these opportunities to maximize revenue by ensuring trucks are always busy. I accomplished that, and then I relaxed and didn't carry on finding more work for trucks because I thought we were doing great.

Boom, nothing stays good forever and that happened where work started to decline, our clients had to use fewer trucks and our trucks were left with no work. When I realized this I hurried to try and get more work but those clients who were taking on trucks for transporting their goods but opportunity had closed and they were not taking on new trucks. Lesson learned; never stop looking for opportunity to grow.

You would think that I learnt from that lesson, I did! My soccer academy which I have been running with just 1 program now has expanded to 1 on 1 home session. We are now going into online training and offering soccer services on the internet.

This process of writing down the reasons of missed opportunities has allowed me to better understand myself. I know which opportunities are for me and which are not. It helped me and it can help you. Think about it, if in 2015 you were missing opportunities and are still missing opportunities currently due to the same reason. My guess is that you aren't doing well economically as cost of living keeps rising. It will be even worse if your income has stayed the same since 2015. Ever heard of how to boils a frog. You don't put into hot water because it will jump out. What you do is put it into warm water in a pot and then you slowly increase the temperature on the stove and the frog will boil to death because it can't detect what's happening. You don't want that to happen to you

I hope I have your attention now that you must put more value on looking for opportunity because it's the gateway to improving your economic condition. If you wrote down your weaknesses in the earlier exercise, then you are aware on how to catch yourself when that pitfall comes up that causes you to constantly miss opportunity. How you respond will completely be different because you will know how to tackle the situation to ensure it's a success. Self sabotage ends there because now you avoid all these pitfalls that you are blind too.

VEHICLES OF OPPORTUNITIES

As we mentioned before to ensure we on the same page, financial freedom is the goal and that R50M in assets which produce 10% monthly passive income. Put your money cap on. Get ready to make sense of the vehicles that available to you. Learn how to take full advantage of them.

Whether you are unemployed, employed, self employed or a businessman, there's always room for improvement to propel yourself forward financially, especially if your income is not passive. Please consider these vehicles and see how quickly they can get you to your destination.

JOB

A job is very important because it provides a stable income which provides stability to cover your necessities through a salary. A job is the first vehicle which can take you from Point A to Point B.

However, how long does it take to get there? Can you currently job get you reach R50M in assets? If yes, how long will it take you there? Here is how a job works, if you start at 20 years old working and stay in the same company for 40 years. Age 60 you retire and then you will have your Pension fund or Provident Fund or Retirement Annuity will be paid out to you as a lump lump of one third, then the two thirds are paid as monthly income for the rest of your retirement provided that you don't outlive your money. So a job offers a form of passive income, but only after 40 years.

Let put this into perspective. Having a job is like walking from DBN to JHB. How long would it take you? (I'm interested to know) what are the dangers that you might encounter along the way? Many people would argue that a promotion makes a difference. Yes that true but that's just going from walking to jogging. It's faster but it's still going to take days.

So maybe having a job is not enough, because and take a closer look at other vehicles of opportunity available to you to ensure that you get to JHB faster.

I see an increasing number of people getting comfortable in their jobs are unwilling to listen and have a look at opportunity. Having an open mind is what's required to you recognize opportunity when it presents itself

SELF EMPLOYMENT OR JOB WITH SIDE HUSTLE

The second vehicle is self employment, and these are often people who have a specialized skill like plumbers, doctors, lawyers, electricians who decide to open up their own company and practice. People using this vehicle tend to make more than people in a job because their income is depended on how many clients are serviced, so it can grow extremely high and a person in a job has a capped income.

What's more popular these days, people have jobs, and then on their spare time they have a side hustle to have an additional source of income, whether it may be selling bags, selling items, consulting etc. They now have a stable income and then an additional source which grows according to how many clients have been serviced or how much they purchased. Having two or three or more income streams definitely makes puts you ahead of a person with just a job and all of a sudden you have more money which get you faster to your goal.

This vehicle is equivalent to driving a car to JHB. You cut days from your trip to hours. Super major improvement, however as good as a car is, you need to attend driving school to learn how to drive. Just like your side hustle requires you to learn specific skills in order to better service your customers. No matter how great the opportunity, the extent to which it works for you depends entirely on your skill set and execution.

This is good place to be in. This where people get stuck because at this point you haven't started making passive income. Your income still requires you to be present in order for it to come. Making the jump to the next vehicle is not hard; it's just that we were not educated on it. So many individuals get trapped here. Why is a trap? Your income also gets s to the point where it's capped due to a time limitation. Eg. If you a plumber and you charge R200 and hour, the only way to increase your revenue is to increase your rate per hour if you are fully booked". The biggest danger here is that if something happened to you, your income stops.

DUPLICATABLE BUSINESS

So let's say you go from using a Corolla to a Ferari, all that does is cut your hours from 6 hours to 4:30 hours. Then you hear that there is something called an "Airplane". Your trip gets cut from hours to thirty minutes. Like with any opportunity, to best utilize it, get skilled. You don't want to crash on your landing when you have arrived at your destination. This is equivalent to the Lottery winner of millions but then ends up broke because he doesn't have the skills to manage that amount of money.

Franchise businesses are the way form of duplicatable business. Why? They don't need the owner directly involved in the operations for it to grow and expand. The likes of KFC, Engen, MacDonalds, Steers etc have a system that allows them to function without own being there allowing him or her to multiply their income because there are multiple branches which bring in income. So you could get a Franchise.

Another option is start your business, focus on creating a system that allows operations to grow without you being directly involved because that opens you up to open another branch which now multiplication starts to work for you. So you have 2 branches giving you income and if you repeat the process long enough you will end up with 20+ branches and that equates to 20 streams of income. Then what most people do when they have accomplished this is sell their companies to investors which give you a nice lump sum. The money

The above examples exclude the person who has a job, practically speaking; franchise requires a lot of money to start off with and starting a traditional business requires lots of money and lots of time which the majority cannot pull off.

There is another duplicatable business which available at low cost of entry, can be done on a part time basis and the revenue unlimited. Robert Kyosaki calls it The Business of the 21st Century which is known as Network

Marketing, another word is Multi Level Marketing. A Network Marketing company comes up with a product or service. When it comes to distributing the product or service, they opt for empowering individuals to distribute the product or service. Company offers the license to individuals to distribute the products or service to other consumers through word of mouth. The company doesn't spend money on mass advertizing but they use that money to reward those distributors according to how much they did.

So an individual signs up with a specific company that sells nutrition products, they sell to another person at R400. That individual makes R100 retail profit because they get the products at a discount which cost him R300. The discount percentage can increase which allows that individual to make more retail profit. The beautiful part of Network Marketing is the second stream of income that gets paid to you when you introduce a person to sign up as a distributor and they purchase the products or sell them. The company will reward you with a percentage of what that member did.

So let's say the company pays you 10% of what your member does. It your member purchases a R1000 worth of products, the company pays you R100. Then after that it becomes a numbers game. The more you add and are active a buying, the more you will earn. This is what we call duplication because that incoming keeps growing when your members are growing.

I have seen people go from making a part time income to making six, seven figures per month doing Network Marketing because there is no limit as to how much you can earn.

Such companies are the likes of Herbalife, Mway, Mary K, World Ventures, IFA, Avon etc.

There is also something called a Pyramid scheme and the difference between the two is this; when there is exchange of money with a promised return and there is no product whether tangible or intangible. That's a pyramid scheme which is illegal. However if there is a product then it's a Network Marketing which is legal.

INCOME PRODUCING ASSETS

If you thought an Airplane is quick. How does a private jet sound? Reaching your destination in 10min and that's the same as having income producing assets which is Real Estate, shares, investments, offshore investments etc. This is the ultimate vehicle to eventually get to. Why? You work so hard create income in the other vehicles. What you need is an asset which will work hard for you. So to graduate here, you simply need to be investing your extra money here.

Here's a game plan to consider: Let's say you working in a job. You learn this information and you decide to get involved in network marketing. So you invest in getting the skills to improve in your job to get promotion and also work your Network Marketing business. So you decide to save R1000 from salary and you also save you retail profit of R2000 per month from your Network Marketing Company. After 12 months you have R36 000 saved. You start attending real estate seminars and after two years, you decide to invest in your first real estate for renting out purposes and you make a net R1000. You savings end up accelerating you keep using it to get more real estate. When you get 50 Real estate Properties which are valued at R1000 000 each paying you R10 000 rent each month. You have reached the goal of R50M in assets which you passive income. You do the maths.

All that's required is to repeat the process over and over and over again until you reach that goal. The game plan is to invest your money in assets you have knowledge in.

Here's the definition of your Financial Freedom "When your lifestyle is paid by the income of your assets and still so much left over"

This is the secret to building generational wealth.

So what's next?

Now that you have the roadmap

WHAT DOES IT TAKE?

"ADAPT OR CHANGE OR JUST DO BOTH"

To get a result that you have never achieved, you have to do something you have never done. You have to change and become a person you have never become. A fool is a person who does the same thing over and over expecting a different result. The crux of the matter here is that you have to change for the better.

Start by committing to change, that means you have to accept failing first and have the courage to work on yourself till the new change within you becomes permanent. This journey requires you to be committed, consistent, focused, disciplined, obsessed, and creative and to always have an expansion mindset. The list is endless with these positive qualities but all is useless if you don't take action because that component guarantees results. Jim Rohn says" Success leaves clues." Tony Robbins wraps it up by saying "to reach success quickly, find a person who has the level of success you want, model what they did".

Remember that these guys worked persistently hard at reaching their level of success but it all started with an Opportunity.

Change is one of the most painful and hard processes you can ever go through because for most of the individuals out, 95% of them have to burn off and some of this bad qualities and habits will scream in agony holding on and not wanting to let go. The harder those negatives hold on in the burning process, the more you should realize that you have to let it go because on the other side, something amazing and powerful within you will blossom. The reborn you will definitely be able to explore more opportunity.

I don't care what you have to give up, if you succeed in that process, you will focus more on opportunity as it's a jealous lover, if you are constantly distracted, then opportunity will leave you and go to another person who give it 100% of their focus. Opportunity wants ALL OF YOU

One more thing to watch out for, when you start changing for the better, life has a funny habit of getting in the way with good or horrible situations. It could be a death in the family, it could be someone close getting sick, it could also be a promotion which takes up all your time that your can't focus on your growth. These things come in all different shapes and form. Life is just testing you and the aim is for you to stay focused on the goal no matter what.

#1 SKILL

Sales, yes it's the S word. Everyone can learn this skill.

Master this skill and you get almost everything you want. I did a course online which involved business. One of the sections was sales and they gave an interesting definition which I could resonate with. That changed my entire perspective on sales as a whole. In the past I didn't like sales because it felt manipulative as I had to use strategies and sales tricks to get a sale. When I found a way to sell without feeling like I was ripping people off, it got me super excited because I go into the sale with a different mindset because sales is all about solving customer problems, that customer wouldn't need your product if they didn't have a problem your product or service can solve.

The greatest products and services solve peoples problem, so my approach is all about solving a problem that the customer has. It was amazing how being upfront with a customer helps, letting them know your intention that my job today is the see if our product or service can solve your problem. If the customer doesn't need your product or service then it ends there with no wasted time. Different spin because it gets to the point, simple, duplicatable and teachable and the best part is that the customer doesn't feel sold after the making a purchase.

Look, there are many forms of selling, truth is that you still have doubts that you do it but it's more natural than you think. If you tell me now that you can't sell, you are selling me on the idea that you can't sell, when you tell me than android is better than Iphone, when you tell me that your team is better than mine, when you tell your friend what they should buy on Black Friday, that's selling. We naturally talk about what happens to us, about the latest upgrades etc yet we don't get compensated for it. We all have the sales skill; it just needs to be nurtured.

Without sales, business dies. Yes I agree that not everyone can be an entrepreneur, but everyone has the potential achieve financial Freedom.

The roadmap has been laid out, especially with the different vehicles. You need to sell yourself on the idea that you need to achieve Financial Freedom and for you to get there, you need to grow your sales skills because it's the one skill that overlaps in your life because you become better negotiator, present yourself better, present a proposal which is well received. That way your influence starts to grow, you become a better leader, better manager, better lover and better friend.

Everyone wants to be better and achieve the above results, but many don't want to learn the skill which is a gateway skill achieving your goals. It's the same as "People want to go to heaven but no one wants to die"

Learn to sell!

How?

You do it…

It's a skill, like a muscle, you can't grow just by thinking about it, reading it about. You have to go out and do it.

It's a number game

The truth about sales is that it's all numbers. Once you do the numbers, you can map out your results once you understand a simple fact that not everyone will buy, however if you know your closing rate then that gives you an idea of how much activity you need to do to achieve your result. If your goal is 10 customers per day, and you understand that for every 5 people you talk to, one agrees to buy. If you do the numbers than you know you have to call 50 customers to get 10 to buy. Beautiful thing about this process is that your closing rate improves to 2 customers buy for every 5 you talk to.

The fortune is in the Follow – up.

I once read a stat which was a game changer, it said, out of 100 potential customers, 2% only bought on the spot and 80% bought after the 6th follow up. That was very interesting because it showed me that I needed to focus on creative ways to follow up because that's when the real money is made.

Respect the odds

When you get better at sales, always remember that not everyone will buy and so don't let your ego get in the way. Know your closing ratio and work according to it.

CONCLUSION

Honest truth is this "we overestimate what we can achieve in a short period of time and we underestimate what we can accomplish over a long period of time". Opportunity is always there, it just requires you be always ready and no matter how lucractive it is. You must be equipped with the relevant skills and knowledge to spot it and take extreme advantage of it.

The beautiful part of this journey is that you can start where you are and with what you got as minimal it may be. When I understood this I had so much hope for the future because I saw where I was on the map and started to chart my course towards my goal and the most rewarding thing is the person I became and trust me, you will also love the person you will become.

"For things to change, you have to change"

Jim Rohn

MY JOURNEY

Thank you so much to if you have stayed with me till you got here. I wrote the book for me as I wanted to figure out where I got lost in my roadmap. I had been stuck for the longest time in the same place financially. I always knew I was missing a piece of the puzzle but just couldn't put my finger on it. Indeed I have found that missing puzzle piece now that has been missing for ages and it was "The real reason why I was stuck where I was" and I hope you were able to find your reason and puzzle piece.

Start where you are, dream big, start small. 2011 when I was doing my second year in university, I took the opportunity to get work experience and I got myself a holiday job in a construction company. Worked there for 2 years, then went to work for a start up transport company. I also worked there for 2 years and then I left to get into Network Marketing. I failed miserably there but I managed to start and register my own company when I didn't have any money or income.

Left my own company to partner up with a colleague in running a transport business, that same year I started a part time soccer academy called "Soccer BootcampSA". After that year I left the transport business to focus on building Soccer BootcampSA full time. Lucky for me in that process I got a flexible job which allowed me to be stable. Soccer bootcampSA grew comfortably.

I always knew Network Marketing is the business for me, and it found me when I had truly bad eating habits. Herbalife Nutrition had amazing products which I fell in love with and I naturally gravitated towards them. After growing my income in network marketing, I left my job to focus on soccer and Network Marketing.

I have a 5 year investment plan with Allan Gray where excess money goes into so that I'm able to invest into income producing assets.

That's a tiny highlight of how I have been taking advantage of opportunity. It hasn't been easy and after completing this book. I'm going to be hit by the toughest challenges ever but I know that I must remained focused on the goal no matter what because Generational Wealth is the goal

Financial freedom is important to everyone and opportunity is the only gateway for you to get there. Think of having a better quality of life, meeting new people who encourage you to do more. When you surround yourself with such people who will stretch you, growth is certain.

APPRECIATION

The person I have become is the one thing I'm truly proud of. I always thought it would be money but money is a validation that what you doing is working. 5 years ago when I began the journey, little did I know who I would eventually become

That's truly attributed by the individuals who were brutally honest with; they pushed me and still are pushing me to be a better person, to grow in life and business.

I just want to truly thank you guys for guiding me. I truly appreciate it I hope that one day I'm able to give back 10x more

YOU GUYS ARE SIMPLY AMAZING HUMAN BEINGS

THANK YOU AND APPRECIATION LIST

1. Ntombizanele Dlamini
2. Nkosinathi Dlamini
3. Shoes Mzi dlamini
4. Bongiwe Dlamini
5. Gary Amstutz
6. Gloria Onie cele
7. Ntombizine Vatiswa Mavume
8. Bonga Mavume
9. Aqua ZS
10. Bernard and Verusia Chetty
11. Byron van Deventer
12. Nococeka Dlamini
13. Blessing Thulani Mcetywa
14. Siyabulela Dlamini
15. Bronwyn Pretorius
16. Robyn and Micheal Sanders
17. Simo Nzama
18. Vukani Mswane
19. Brett and Kelly Yeatman

20. Forest Hills Sports club and members

21. Soccer BootcampSA parents and kids

22. Herbalife team and Focus Team

23. Starbucks Colleagues

24. RubberstampSA Team

25. Friends (Throwback, WayForward, Amajimboz)

26. Dlamini, Mahlobo & Mbhele family

FIND ME

FACEBOOK PAGES: NKOSI MPHILE "NK24" DLAMINI

NK24 NKOSI DLAMINI

SOCCERBOOTCAMPSA

SESSY EVENTS AND DÉCOR

INSTAGRAM: @OPPORTUNITYWITHNK24

@SOCCERBOOTCAMPSA

EMAIL ADDRESS: NDAMINI6@GMAIL.COM

www.ingramcontent.com/pod-product-compliance
Lightning Source LLC
Chambersburg PA
CBHW030535220526
45463CB0C007B/2840